I LIKE TO LOOK FOR
RAINBOWS

Cover design © 2016 by Covenant Communications, Inc.
Cover and interior illustrations © Beth M. Whittaker

Words and Music © Nita Dale Milner

Published by Covenant Communications, Inc., American Fork, Utah

Printed in South Korea
Production Date:
Production Location:
Job / Batch #

First Printing: September 2016
7/8/2016
WeSP, Paju-si, Gyeonggi-do, South Korea
67490

22 21 20 19 18 17 16   10 9 8 7 6 5 4 3 2 1

ISBN-13: 978-1-68047-643-9

I LIKE TO LOOK FOR
RAINBOWS

Illustrations by Beth M. Whittaker
Words and Music by Nita Dale Milner

I like to look
for rainbows

whenever there is rain

And ponder on the beauty

of an earth
made clean again.

I want my life to be as clean
as earth right after rain.

I want to be the best I can

and live with God again.

I know when I am baptized

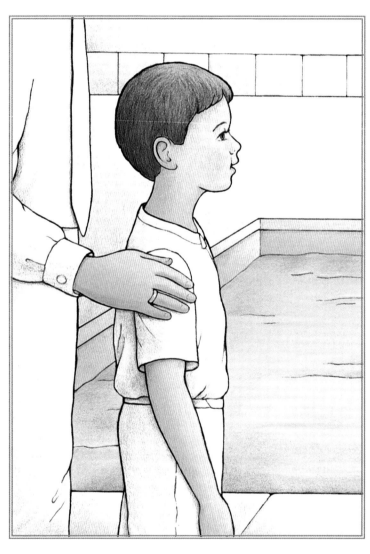

my wrongs are washed away,

And I can be forgiven

and improve myself each day.

I want my life to be as clean
as earth right after rain.

I want to be the best I can

and live with God again.

When I Am Baptized

Thoughtfully ♩ = 60–72

1. I like to look for rain-bows when-ev-er there is rain And pon-der on the beau-ty of an earth made clean a - gain.

2. I know when I am bap-tized my wrongs are washed a - way, And I can be for-giv-en and im - prove my-self each day.

Chorus

I want my life to be as clean as earth right af - ter rain. I want to be the best I can and live with God a - gain.

Words: Nita Dale Milner, b. 1952; adapted. © 1989 LDS
Music: Nita Dale Milner, b. 1952, © 1989 LDS

Genesis 9:8–17
Acts 2:38